# The Odd 1s Out

# JOURNAL

## JAMES RALLISON

A TarcherPerigee Book

**tarcher**perigee

an imprint of Penguin Random House LLC
penguinrandomhouse.com

Most TarcherPerigee books are available at special quantity discounts for bulk
purchase for sales promotions, premiums, fund-raising, and educational needs.
Special books or book excerpts also can be created to fit specific needs.
For details, write: SpecialMarkets@penguinrandomhouse.com.

Trade paperback ISBN: 9780593539460

Printed in the United States of America
1st Printing

# INTRODUCTION

The only reason we know history happened was because someone alive at the time wrote down that day's events. And yeah, we're at the most-documented point in human history with the internet and all, but who knows what the future holds? Maybe this journal will be the only thing that's preserved in the upcoming millennium, and future archaeologists will use it as the next Rosetta stone. In that case, you better write everything in three different languages just to be safe.

But even if your journal isn't put in a museum, it can still be used as a personal record book—a window into what your own history looked like. The whole appeal of journals is to write in them at a younger age and then look back on them with an older and more developed brain with the power of retrospect. Or there's a possibility that you'll use this journal to keep your grocery list, which I guess is useful, too, but I doubt it will end up in any future museums. So start filling out these pages with anything you want. No idea is a bad one. The important thing is that you get it on paper.

its no

Start the journal with a bucket list. They're always the most fun to look back on and feel either accomplished or disappointed.

o<sub></sub>

name: Julian. age: 7
height: 4 feet

name: SOFIA

age: 11

height: 5'0

my mom wakes me up super early. I get redy for school. my mom drivese me and mt big sister to school. I start school. school ends. I eat I do nothing the day ends. I sleep. the day repets

I got to school hang out "centers" where we technadly do nothing then we read 1-2 chapters of Hunger Games then go to MR. Luna's class which is "math" but we only do olps, P.E. more olps, a chapter of Hunger Games then school ends

**What does an average day look like for your pet? (If you have no pets, what WOULD an average day look like for your dream pet?)**

walk around, eat, sleep

its repets

well i have two, with VERY different personalities, it's, Finn & Jake. Finn is my cat and ~~Jac~~ Jake is my brother's. Jake is usally more energetic than Finn & goes out more. So below is a schedule

| Finn's day | Jakes day |
|---|---|
| - stay up all night | |
| - eat sleep | Same thing |
| - ~~go~~ out | |

Do you have a best friend? What about them made you
want to be their friend?

he had blue, red orang hair
he was funny, he talked to
me, we met sige 1st grade.

NOPE. (no bff) lol

5

Dear Diary, today I buried
my uncle

did nothing exept for this

Anything funny happen recently that you don't want to forget? Immortalize that hilarious experience below.

I said we are orange table with an orange

no nothing :(

If you could be friends with anyone in the world, who would you choose?

Devon Bostick

Gael Aular-Gomez
Halle bailey ♡

Felix g⊙

Two trains are driving toward each other. The first train leaves Town A at 5 a.m. traveling at 60 miles per hour. The second train leaves Town B at 7 a.m. traveling at 70 miles per hour. The distance between Town A and Town B is 455 miles.

What is the EXACT time that the collision will occur?

## What is your earliest memory?

when right
after
my friend
got picked up
I got picked
up ;-)

10

What's something you've done that not a lot of other people have done?

IDK?

Slade baths

# What superpower do you wish you had, and what would you do with it?

tuhn invis. Scnare feels

CONTROL TIME!
(cause i could go back to
my best days :))

What inventions do you think the world still needs?

Spork → Stork

a ball pit with prizes

Cantrd time
Watch

13

If you could time travel, what would you say to your past self? What would you say to your future self?

Past= say peace to Somore
Futyre = watch my nihtendo

Past: dont waste
your energy
on some one with
bad energy mdo:

future: try hard for me.

What's something that you've already done that you never want to do again? (This list will grow the older you get, so leave lots of room.)

try to float. try to be funny.
did not end well

# What was the last thing that made you laugh?

my Mom

I was going to ~~skate alone~~ going to take the trash out

If you could relive one day, which would it be, and why?

when me & D (LIFYKYK)
were close & hugged

Where do you think you'll be living in fifteen years? How did you get there?

prob in an apartment in like NYC

Do you think you're an introvert or an extrovert?
Why?

IM none m
in the middle

What's the nicest thing anyone has ever done for you?

given me
a whole
PRIME

give me gushers

Kaden

The best thing about being my age is:

you get to
go to elementry
4 a while

The worst thing about being my age is:

*(handwritten scribbles)*

23

Hydration check! Have you drunk enough water today? If you're thirsty, then you're already dehydrated! Oh, you still need a prompt? What's the best part about being hydrated?

What are your talents? It doesn't have to be something big, like you're a gold-medal-winning gymnast or something. Are you double-jointed? Can you wiggle your ears? Share, please!

What talent do you wish you had? (Do you want it enough to practice said talent?)

be able to play guitar

Some people believe there are other universes just like ours. If this is true, what do you think your other selves are doing right now?

one of them for sure are taking a huge 8hit on the toilet

:)

Does this book smell good? What does it smell like?

It smells like
a book

What . . . what do you smell like? (Be honest.)

Sometimes like ~~crap~~ Crap

but mostly "Sol Janairo"

Are you psychic? Let's find out. Write five predictions
for things that will happen this month. Come back to
this page in thirty days to see if you were right.

- some one ~~xxxxxx~~ will confess to me
- graduation will be perfect
- Mr. Lorenzo will cry on the last day, lol
- I will get lots of ~~our~~ gifts

~~morning~~

- the plan we have w/ ariana will go great

Write a letter to a relative you haven't spoken to in a while and then tear out this page and send it to them. (Standard postage rates may apply.)

What's something that you used to hate when you were younger but now you love? (Have you given Brussels sprouts another try? No, really, they're amazing if you roast them.)

I bet you can't draw a self-portrait with your nondominant hand.

What would you want to see in the museum
of your life?

my fav
person
Satue

34

You're a celebrity! What are you famous for?

my acting

35

Think fast! Draw the first thing that comes to mind that starts with the letter M.

mandirin

1st
MOM, moth 2nd
mouse 3rd

Where would you go on your dream vacation? Who's
coming with you?

Italy

& i would
take
DAVID
G + clawi
lala
yasmin

Write about your day from the perspective of your pet or dream pet.

Who is someone you admire? Why?

pepe cause
hes smart

If you started a YouTube channel, what would you make videos about?

VLOGS

What is your favorite joke? If you can't remember it, make one up right now!

Make an acronym from your name and then illustrate what you came up with. (Example: Jellyfish And Marshmallows Exist Separately. Sure, it doesn't make sense, but it's my name!)

Sour Sally Cooked

If you could create a mythical creature or monster, what would it look like? Try drawing it here.

# Do you collect anything? Is there anything you want to start collecting?

Do you prefer dressing up or staying in your pajamas?
(I work from home, so it's pajamas all day for me.)

dressing up

Write about the last birthday you had.
Did you enjoy it?

my 12th

If you had twenty-four hours to spend $1 million, what would you spend it on, and what names would you give all the puppies you're going to adopt?

Id Spend it
on a house

What's something you think is a scam?

What's a topic you could rant about for hours?
(Start this prompt with, "Don't get me started on
_____" and then proceed to get started.)

Do you watch anime with subtitles or
dubbed over with English?

dubbed

Which pet would you want? A blue turtle that shoots water, a red lizard with fire at the end of its tail, or a grass type?

# Which Harry Potter house do you belong in? Why?

Ravenclaw

At what point did math become confusing for you?

2nd

If a tree falls in a forest and no one is there to hear it, does it make a sound?

Name three things that you think you and I have in common. (If you don't know me personally, just make some assumptions.)

# Why should I hire you?

Why not?

# What's the best compliment you've ever received?

"ur pretty!"

When was the last time you complimented someone?

ántier

# What's the real reason Pepsi Next was discontinued?

I havent
watched lots of scary
movies
but prob

"Fear Street"

# What was the worst haircut you've ever received, and who cut it?

# Are you a domesticated wolf or a domesticated lion person?

What's the fastest mile you've ever run? (My fastest mile is not that good, either.)

Have you ever broken a bone, or do you drink a lot of milk and have strong bones?

# Find the area of this shape.
## (Remember, area = length x width.)

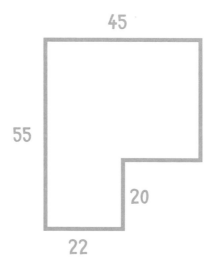

45

55

20

22

What model was your first cell phone? How old were you when you got it?

I got
~~an~~ a samsung glaxy
21 or somethin
like that and
I was like 9 or 8

If you could make it rain something other than water, what would you change the rain to?

What's a sound that makes you cringe every time you hear it?

?

# What is your favorite YouTube/TikTok video?

Would you care if your parents started a family vlogging channel starring you and everything that goes on in your life?

Sure

TEOTFW

cause I LOVE It

How are you preparing for the zombie apocalypse?
(I don't think I would survive that long,
if I'm being honest.)

If you could live in a video game, which one would you want to live in?

animal crossing

What animal or bug are you glad DOESN'T have wings?

*cúkarachas*

If you were an animal, what animal would you be?

dog

What do you think updog looks like? Draw your imaginings here. (If you don't know what updog is, ask someone.)

Scenario: The famous ship sailed by the hero Theseus in a great battle was kept in a harbor as a memorial. As time passed, some of the wooden parts began to rot and were replaced with new ones. Within 100 years, every part had been replaced. With all new parts, can we consider the "restored" ship to be the same ship as the original?

Furthermore, let's say that the pieces that had been removed were stored in a warehouse, and later on, technology was developed that cured the rot and enabled the pieces to be reassembled into a ship. Is this "reconstructed" ship the original ship? What about the restored one—is that still the same as the original? Can they both be considered the original ship?

Hey, here's a more simple question: Why?

Aside from a pot of gold, what would you want to find at the end of a rainbow?

CANDY

and
1 mil dollars

What's something parents just don't understand?

It's been a while since you checked in on your New Year's resolutions, huh? How well are you accomplishing them? (If you don't do New Year's resolutions, what are some you can think of right now?)

# What's one thing you'd change about the internet?

If you could bring one book, one video game, and one movie to a deserted island, what would you bring?

The Odd 1s Out

What are your favorite "Would You Rather" questions?

Do you remember a time when you lost at a game but handled it very well? If you can't think of an example, write a few things you can work on in the future.

If your toys were sentient like in *Toy Story*, what would they be doing when you're not home?

True or false: This statement is false. Explain your reasoning below.

The object to your left has come alive and is trying to kill you. How much trouble are you in?

LOTS

If an apple a day keeps the doctor away, what keeps dentists away?

Have you ever messed up trying to cook something?
What was your mistake? Have you tried
making it again?

Have you ever been to a convention? If you haven't, what convention would you like to go to?

What is the best present you've ever received?

# What is the best present you've ever given?

# What are some classes taught at dog school?

Why did the chicken cross the road?

What's one question you wish people would
stop asking?

# What's something that's not meant to be scary but still frightens you?

# What do you spend the most money on?

the mall. lol.

What's the most boring fact you know, and where did you learn it?

# If you were invisible for a day, what would you do?

Steel

What's something that reminds you of "the good ol' days"?

# What was the best prank you've ever pulled? Plan your next one here.

If you could spend the day with any cartoon character, who would it be?

Finn the human ♡ ♡

Of all the animals on Earth, which one is most likely an alien?

If you could make a movie based on a book or video game, what movie would you make, and who would you cast in the lead role?

~~Seth Rogan~~

november 9th

cast
fallon: emma Stone?
ryle: Devon Bostick

What's the longest line you remember waiting in?
Was it worth it?

Did you do the science fair in school? What was your science question, and what was it like? If your school wasn't run by psychopaths, what would you want to do a science project about?

Which conspiracy theory do you believe? Which one do you want to be true?

# What are the ingredients to the perfect sandwich?

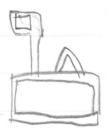

What was it like growing up as the youngest/middle/
oldest/only child?

What do you miss most about the year 2015?

What misconception did you believe for a long time?

What's a misconception people have about you?

Would you be friends with your parents if they were the same age as you?

my mom YES dad mabye

# What would you do with a time machine?

# What food will you never get tired of eating?

# What are your least and most favorite Halloween candies?

Would you rather be rich and dumb or
poor and smart?

Poor

Poor

If you could go on any reality show, what show would you want to be on?

What is the most recent app that you downloaded? Why did you download it?

What is the strangest candle scent that you would buy? (That's a weird way of asking: What strange smells do you enjoy?)

If the movie *Inside Out* were true, what would be some of your core memories?

What's something you would do if you weren't afraid?

## What song have you been listening to on repeat recently?

Sunset Rollercoaster - my Jinji.

What's the strangest thing you have in your notes app?

They say there's no such thing as a stupid question, but what are some stupid questions?

What are some YouTube rabbit holes that you've fallen down? (If you haven't been down any, I recommend looking up candy-pulling videos.)

# What is the most unexplainable thing that has happened to you?

# What do you think the worst roommate acts like?

# What was the best thing you ever bought that was under $10?

# What dream do you remember vividly?

What do you do to stay healthy? (Alternative version of this question: What do you do when you're not on your phone?)

What activity makes you lose track of time?

# Who do you love, and what are you doing about it?

If you had to teach something, what would you teach?

# Which is worse, failing or never trying?

What would you say if you could talk to everyone in the world at the same time?

If you could make an author rewrite the ending of their book, which book would you pick?

# Do you live in Oklahoma? Why?

What's the funniest thing you said as a toddler?

What would you do if you found out you had an evil twin?

# Xbox, PlayStation, or the good one (Nintendo)?

What's heavier, a kilogram of steel or a pound of feathers?

What event would you like to see added to the
Olympics? (It does not have to be a sport.)

Is cereal a soup? Justify your answer below.

# What's your favorite movie with a penguin in it?

What's an activity you have always wanted to try but feel you might be made fun of for attempting it?

If you could talk to one person, dead or alive, who
would you talk to, and what would you ask?

If your life was a novel, what would be the title, and how would your story end?

What book, movie, or video game makes you angry?
Why does it make you angry?

# How has your life changed in the last three years?

What are some of the recurring meals at your house?
Do you like eating them?

If you could choose how the world will end, what would you pick? Describe your ideal apocalypse.

What's something that you begged your parents to buy but then only used once?

If you could eat only three things for the rest of your life, what would they be?

# What is something you tried this year that you've never done before?

If a trolley was about to hit a group of five people, but you could pull a lever and divert the trolley to hit just one person, would you? Would your answer change if the one person was young and the group of five were elderly?

# Do you believe in astrology? Why or why not?

* Whats YOUR *
* Sign? +

If you discovered a new species of dinosaur, what would you name it, and what would it look like? Draw the specimen here.

# What is something that makes you feel at home?

# What new feature would you like added to the next iPhone?

What do you think is something that everyone can agree on?

Have you ever gone camping? Where did you go, and did you enjoy it?

What's something that used to be super popular but now seems like everyone has forgotten about?